Gospel Primer

THE

GOSPEL PRIMER

"And that from a child thou hast known the Holy Scriptures, which are able to make thee wise unto salvation through faith which is in Christ Jesus." 2 Tim. 3:15.

Thirty-eighth Edition — 527th Thousand.

REVIEW AND HERALD PUBLISHING COMPANY,

BATTLE CREEK, MICHIGAN,

CHICAGO, ILL., ... ATLANTA, GA.

1900.

LIST OF ILLUSTRATIONS.

	PAGE
Frontispiece	..
The Earth at Creation	38
The Tower of Babel	42
The Selling of Joseph	46
Joseph Interpreting Pharaoh's Dream	48
Joseph's Dream	52
Jacob Going Down to Egypt	56
Bringing Water from the Rock	62
Israelites Gathering Manna	64
Elijah's Offering	68
The Handwriting on the Wall	70
The Three Hebrews before the King	74
In the Fiery Furnace	76
The Wise Men Presenting Gifts to Jesus	80
Flight into Egypt	82
Jesus among the Doctors	84
Turning Water into Wine	88
Jesus Raising Jairus' Daughter	92
Jesus Healing the Sick	94
The Sea of Galilee	95
Jesus Feeding the Five Thousand	96
The Fire by the Sea	100
The Blind Beggar	102
Ruins of the Pool of Siloam	105
Jesus Blessing Little Children	106
The Disciples Plucking Corn	110
Jesus and the Woman of Samaria	112
Jesus Riding into Jerusalem	120
The Crucifixion	122
The Ascension	124
A Little Child Shall Lead Them	126

COPYRIGHTED 1896 BY INTERNATIONAL TRACT SOCIETY. All Rights Reserved.

CONTENTS.

	PAGE
A B C and Slate Exercise	7
Word Method	16
The Creation	39
The Confusion of Tongues	41
The Favorite Son	44
Faithfulness Rewarded	49
Joseph's Dream Fulfilled	53
Brotherly Love Restored	57
Water from the Rock	61
Bread from Heaven	65
Elijah and the Priests of Baal	67
The Handwriting on the Wall	71
The Three Hebrews and the Fiery Furnace	73
The Birth of Jesus	79
Jesus and the Doctors in the Temple	85
Turning Water into Wine	87
The Raising of Jairus' Daughter	91
Jesus Feeds the Five Thousand	97
The Fire by the Sea	99
Jesus Heals the Blind Beggar	103
Jesus Blessing Little Children	107
The Sabbath Made for Man	109
Jesus at Jacob's Well	113
The Need of Prayer	116
Jesus Riding into Jerusalem	119
The Ascension	123
A Little Child Shall Lead Them	127

Learning to Read.

THERE are two quite distinct ways of teaching beginners to read. In the alphabetic method, the letters are first learned, and then built into words. With this method nearly every one is familiar.

In the word method, certain words are first learned, and then built into simple sentences. This method has the advantage of giving the learner something at the outset that can suggest thought and awaken interest.

In this primer, facilities are furnished for both methods. The alphabet is presented in very attractive form, and then follows the word method, beginning on page sixteen.

In teaching by the word method, the teacher does not try to teach the letters at first. He begins with words. For example, take the first lesson on page sixteen. First teach the word "God" till it can be recognized anywhere; then the word "good," and the word "is." Then the first sentence can be read,—"God is good." Then by adding "am" and "I" the next sentence can be read. Add "love," and we may read, "God is love." In this way the whole lesson may soon be read.

The second lesson contains no new words except those put in bold type below it, and so with every lesson. We need be in no hurry about the alphabet; for nearly all children will learn it incidentally before reading very far in this way.

It is a good practice to have the learner print the most prominent words on a slate or on paper. The words in bold type afford a good spelling lesson, for either oral or written spelling exercises.

GOSPEL PRIMER

A is for Adam, who was the first man.

(SLATE EXERCISE.)

the   man   for
first   Adam   is

"So God created man in his own image, in the image of God created he him."   Genesis 1 : 27.

B is for Bethlehem, where Jesus was born.

(SLATE EXERCISE.)

was   for   is   born
where   Jesus

"Now when Jesus was born in Bethlehem of Judæa, in the days of Herod the king, behold, there came wise men from the east to Jerusalem."   Matthew 2 : 1.

C is for Cain, who killed his brother.

(SLATE EXERCISE.)

killed   brother

who   his   for

"And it came to pass, when they were in the field, that Cain rose up against Abel his brother, and slew him." Genesis 4:8.

D is for Daniel, who was cast into the lion's den.

(SLATE EXERCISE.)

cast   was   lion

into   den

"Then the king commanded, and they brought Daniel, and cast him into the den of lions." Daniel 6:16.

E is for Elijah, who was taken to heaven.

(SLATE EXERCISE.)

heaven   taken   was

to   for   is

"Behold, there appeared a chariot of fire, and horses of fire; . . . . . and Elijah went up by a whirlwind into heaven." 2 Kings 2:11.

 is for flood, that drowned the world.

(SLATE EXERCISE.)

flood world that drowned for the

"And, behold, I, even I, do bring a flood of waters upon the earth, to destroy all flesh, wherein is the breath of life." Genesis 6:17.

 is for the giant Goliath, who was slain by David.

(SLATE EXERCISE.)

slain giant for David was

"And David said to Saul, Let no man's heart fail because of him; thy servant will go and fight with this Philistine." 1 Samuel 17:32.

 is for Hannah, who gave her son Samuel to the Lord.

(SLATE EXERCISE.)

Lord son gave Samuel who

She "brought the child to Eli. Therefore also I have lent him to the Lord; as long as he liveth he shall be lent to the Lord." 1 Samuel 1:25-28.

 **I** is for Isaac, the son of Abraham.

(SLATE EXERCISE.)

Isaac   son   of
for   is   the

"Take now thy son, thine only son Isaac, whom thou lovest, and get thee into the land of Moriah; and offer him there for a burnt offering." Genesis 22:2.

 **J** is for Jacob, to whom the angels appeared in a dream.

(SLATE EXERCISE.)

dream   angels   the
whom   Jacob

"And he dreamed, and, behold, a ladder set up on the earth, and the top of it reached to heaven; and, behold, the angels of God ascending and descending on it." Genesis 28:12.

 **K** is for Korah, who was swallowed up by the earth.

(SLATE EXERCISE.)

earth   up   by   the
who   was   is

"And the earth opened her mouth, and swallowed them up." Numbers 16:32.

 is for Lazarus, whom Christ raised from the dead.

(SLATE EXERCISE.)

Christ raised the from dead

"And when he thus had spoken, he cried with a loud voice, Lazarus, come forth." John 11:43.

 is for Methuselah, the oldest man.

(SLATE EXERCISE.)

man oldest the is for

"And all the days of Methuselah were nine hundred sixty and nine years; and he died." Genesis 5:27.

 is for Nazareth, the home of Jesus.

(SLATE EXERCISE.)

Jesus of home for the is

"And he came and dwelt in a city called Nazareth." Matthew 2:23.

O is for Olivet, the mount on which Jesus prayed.

(SLATE EXERCISE.)

mount   for   which

prayed   on

"And he came out, and went, as he was wont, to the Mount of Olives." Luke 22 : 39.

P is for Pharaoh, who was drowned in the Red Sea.

(SLATE EXERCISE.)

drowned   sea   in

who   was   is

"And the waters returned, and covered the chariots, and the horsemen, and all the host of Pharaoh." Exodus 14 : 28.

Q is for Queen of Sheba, who visited Solomon.

(SLATE EXERCISE.)

Queen   who   for

visited   Solomon

" And when the Queen of Sheba heard of the fame of Solomon, concerning the name of the Lord, she came to prove him with hard questions." 1 Kings 10 : 1.

 is for Rome, where Paul was put in prison.

(SLATE EXERCISE.)

Paul put prison where Rome

"And when we came to Rome, the centurion delivered the prisoners to the captain of the guard; but Paul was suffered to dwell by himself, with a soldier that kept him." Acts 28:16.

 is for Sodom, the city destroyed by fire.

(SLATE EXERCISE.)

city destroyed by for the fire

"Then the Lord rained upon Sodom, and upon Gomorrah, brimstone and fire." Genesis 19:24.

 is for Troas, where Paul preached all night.

(SLATE EXERCISE.)

night all where preached Paul

"When he .... had broken bread, and eaten, and talked a long while, even till break of day, so he departed." Acts 20:11.

U is for Uzzah, who steadied the ark.

(SLATE EXERCISE.)

ark for steadied
who is the

"Uzzah put forth his hand to the ark of God, and took hold of it; for the oxen shook it. And God smote him there for his error." 2 Samuel 6:6, 7.

V is for vine, which represents Christ.

(SLATE EXERCISE.)

Christ for vine
which represents

"I am the vine, ye are the branches." John 15:5.

W is for watchman, on the walls of Zion.

(SLATE EXERCISE.)

Zion walls of
for the on

"Watchman, what of the night? The watchman said, The morning cometh, and also the night." Isaiah 21:11. 12.

 is for Xerxes (Ahasuerus), King of Persia.

(SLATE EXERCISE.)

Persia is of king for

"Now it came to pass in the days of Ahasuerus, ... he made a feast unto all his princes .... of Media and Persia." Esther 1 : 1–3.

 is for the yoke of Christ.

(SLATE EXERCISE.)

Christ of for yoke is the

"My yoke is easy, and my burden is light." Matthew 11 : 30.

 is for Zion, the home of the blest.

(SLATE EXERCISE.)

Zion blest the home of for

"And I looked, and lo, a lamb stood on the Mount Zion, and with him an hundred forty and four thousand." Revelation 14:1.

WORD-METHOD.

GOD IS LOVE.

God. Good.—God is good. Am I good? God is love. He loves me. Do I love God?

Men.—Good men. Good men love God. God loves all men. Do all men love God?

God is good to all men. He is good to me.

| God | good | all | am | to | I |
| love | men | me | is | do | he |

MOTHER LOVE.

Mother.—The mother. The good mother. The good mother loves God, and God loves her.

Child.—The child. The good child. The child is good. The good child loves his mother.

My mother is good to me. I am my mother's child. Do I love my mother? If I love her, I will be good to her.

| Mother | her | his | my | the |
| child | the | him | will | if |

BROTHER LOVE.

Brother. — My brother. My good brother. My brother loves me. He is good to me.

Sister. Dear. — My sister. My dear sister. She is good to me. My sister loves her mother and her brother.

My sister is my mother's child, and so is my brother. Our mother loves all her children, and we love her.

All good children love their mother.

Brother	children	dear	our	their
sister	and	so	we	man

FATHER LOVE.

Father. — Our dear father. Our father is a good man. He loves my mother, and she loves him.

Our father loves his children, and they all love him. He is a good father to us, and we will all be good children.

Heaven. Who. — God is our Father in heaven. All who love him are his children. He loves them more than father or mother can love their children.

God loves my father and my mother. He loves my brother and my sister. He loves me. If I love God, I will love my brothers and sisters.

| Father | who | us | are | more |
| heaven | they | in | can | than |

THE HAPPY HOME.

Happy. — My father and mother are God's children. They love him, and he loves them.

Home. — Our home is a happy home. Our father and mother love their children, and love each other. Their children love them, and love one another.

Makes. — Love makes us happy. We love God and one another; so he puts his love upon us.

No home can be happy without love. In heaven all is love. If it were not so, heaven would not be a happy place.

Happy	each	one	them	puts
without	place	other	another	makes
upon	home	would	were	

THE HOME IN EDEN.

Adam. First. Woman. Eve.—Adam was the first man, and Eve was the first woman.

Beautiful. Place. Made. Live.—God made Adam and Eve, and made a beautiful place for them to live in.

Very. Loved.—They were very happy; for they loved God, and they loved each other. All who love God are happy.

Garden. Eden. Trees. Flowers.—This beautiful place was the Garden of Eden. And Eden was like heaven. All was love, and all was beautiful,—the trees, the birds, the flowers.

Talked. Walked.—And God was in the garden with them, and talked with them, and walked with them.

Adam	first	live	very	like
Eve	place	loved	garden	trees
woman	made	beautiful	Eden	flowers
walked	talked	with	birds	

EDEN LOST.

Adam and Eve were happy in Eden as long as they loved God more than they loved to have their own way.

They were glad to obey him. He knew better than they did what was good for them,

and what would make them happy.

But by and by bad thoughts came into their minds. Their own way seemed better to them than God's way. Then the love of God went out of them, and they did not obey him.

But they were not happy any more. They were ashamed to see God, and when he came into the garden, they hid among the trees.

Long	obey	would	came	ashamed
own	knew	minds	seemed	when
way	better	bad	then	among
have	what	thoughts	went	hid

SIN AND SORROW.

All the way down, from the time when Adam and Eve sinned in the Garden of Eden and had to go out of it, men have been making themselves unhappy in the same way.

To disobey God is to sin. If no one had

ever sinned, then no one would ever have died.

If all who have ever lived had loved God and one another, they would all have been happy.

If no one had ever sinned, there would be no sickness, no sorrow, no graves.

What bad work sin has made! . If we sin, it will make sorrow for us.

Down	time	sinned	been	making
themselves	ever	sorrow	died	had
lived	sickness	graves	work	disobey

OUR HOPE.

We have all gone wrong sometimes. We have not always walked in the way that God has marked out.

When we have gone in our own way, we have made ourselves unhappy. We have let the love of God go out and the love of self come in. In all this we have shut out the God who loves us. We have made our own sorrows.

We have to bear the sins of others, too; for we would have to be sick and die, even if we did not sin.

But God will forgive our sins. He will give us good thoughts. He will help us to love him, and to love one another. We must die, but we shall live again; and in that life all will be happiness, and love, and peace.

There we shall never sin, and never die. We shall never be sick, and never be sad. We shall be more and more happy forever and ever.

Gone	marked	bear	help	peace
wrong	ourselves	would	must	sad
sometimes	self	even	shall	never
always	come	give	again	forever

EDEN REGAINED.

God loves men too well to leave them in sorrow always. Sin leads to death, but men shall live again.

God so loved men, even sinful men, that he  gave his own Son to die for them, so that they could have a new life after death.

Jesus, the Son of God, was put to death; but God brought him to life again, and took him to heaven.

God's children will take Jesus for their Saviour. They will love him and obey him; and the time will come when "all that are in their graves shall come forth."

Then God will take his children to heaven, and give them a home more beautiful than the Eden where Adam and Eve were so happy.

There they will see God. Jesus will be there, and so will all the good people who have ever lived.

There will be no sin there, and their joy will never end.

Well	death	could	Jesus	took
where	joy	leave	sinful	new
Saviour	see	end	there	people
leads	son	after	brought	forth

THE REDEEMER'S LOVE.

In heaven Jesus, the Son of God, was above all the angels. He was more beautiful than any of them, and was next to his Father in honor and glory.

But he was full of pity for the unhappy children of men. He loved them, and was willing to give up the glory of heaven, and come to the earth.

God sent his Son to the earth in the form of a child, a baby in his mother's arms. He

came to earth to show us how to obey God,—
how to live so as to do good in this life, and
be happy in the life to come.

He came as a child, so as to show children
how to live. He came like other children, and
grew up as other children do, only better and
wiser.

He knew that bad men would not love him,
and that they would at last put him to death.
But his love for men is great, and he said to
his Father, "Lo, I come to do thy will."

Above	glory	willing	pity	baby
only	great	angels	earth	sent
arms	wiser	said	honor	next
full	form	grew	last	thy

THE LOWLY ONE.

When God sent his Son to the earth, he gave
him into the care of two good people who lived
in Nazareth.

Joseph and Mary worked hard for a living.
Their home was humble, but it was a happy one.

When Jesus came to them, they were in
Bethlehem. They had gone there on a journey.
There was no room for them in the inn, so they
had to stay in a place made for cattle.

They could be happy in any place; for they loved God. They knew, too, that he loved them.

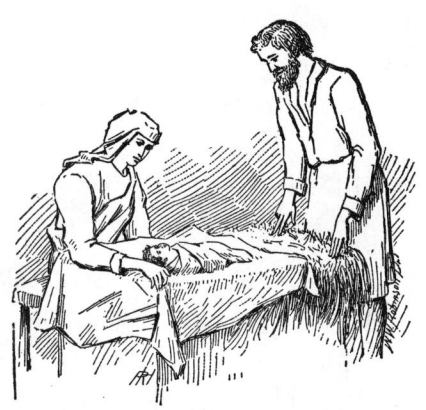

They knew that God would give his Son Jesus to them, to be cared for till he should grow up.

They knew that God had a care for them. He sent angels to watch over them on their journey. Angels were with them in the humble place where they slept.

God was not ashamed to give his Son to the care of poor people. He was not ashamed to have him born in a stable, and cradled in a manger.

Nazareth	hard	journey	stay	over
poor	cradled	living	Joseph	Bethlehem
cattle	watch	slept	stable	manger
	Mary	room	inn	

GOD MAKES KNOWN HIS SON.

On the very night when Jesus was born in Bethlehem, good shepherds were watching their flocks not far away. While they were watching, they saw a company of angels. At first they were afraid of the glory,— a glory bright as the sun.

But an angel came near, and talked to them. He told them to go to Bethlehem, where they would find the Son of God, — a babe in a manger.

Then the angels all sang praises to God, and went away. It was good news that the angels brought. Jesus, the Son of God, had come to earth. He was then in Bethlehem. They could go there and see him.

They were full of joy, and when they had seen the child Jesus, they went away praising God. They believed what the angels had said to them, and told every one they met that they had seen the Saviour of men.

Night	far	company	news	every
shepherds	saw	bright	full	met
born	sun	praises	believed	flocks
one	went	brought	Saviour	

THE DUTIFUL SON.

God took good care that all should know that the child Jesus was the Christ. He had his prophets tell it in the temple, and he made it known to the wise men of the East.

Bad men tried to put the child to death. But God kept him out of their power.

Jesus lived with Joseph and Mary in Nazareth. It was a beautiful place among the hills. There were birds and brooks, trees and flowers. And above all were the great rocks.

But the people of Nazareth were many of them bad. They did not love God. They did not care to obey him. But Jesus did not join with them in their bad ways.

He helped Joseph and Mary at home. He obeyed them in all things, though he knew what a great work he would have to do by and by. In everything, he showed how a good child should live.

It was not hard for Jesus to do this; for he loved every one, and love makes all things easy.

Christ	prophets	temple	East	tried
kept	power	easy	things	hills
rocks	great	many	helped	obeyed

THE HEAVENLY DOVE.

Jesus stayed with Joseph and Mary in Nazareth till he was thirty years old. The time had then come for him to go out and talk to the people.

His cousin John, who was a little older than Jesus, had been for some time telling the people to turn away from their sins. He taught them to love one another and to love God.

He told them that Jesus, the Christ, was coming. Those that believed and obeyed were baptized by John in the river Jordan.

One day Jesus came to be baptized. John knew that Jesus had never sinned, and that he did not need to be baptized. But Jesus would set a good example for others, and so John baptized him.

When Jesus came up out of the water, the Holy Spirit came down in the form of a dove, and rested upon him. The dove is an emblem of love. The Holy Spirit is the Spirit of God, and God is love. Jesus, like his Father, is also love. He so loved men that he was willing to give his life for them. He loves them just the same now.

But this was not all. God spoke from heaven, and said, "This is my beloved Son."

Thirty	cousin	telling	Jordan	Holy
years	little	taught	need	Spirit
old	just	baptized	example	emblem
till	some	river	dove	beloved

DOING GOOD.

After Jesus was baptized, he went about doing good. While he was at Cana, near Nazareth, a nobleman came to see him. He had heard how Jesus had healed many sick people, and had done many wonderful things.

This nobleman had a dear son at home, who was sick and nigh unto death.

The more they did for him, the worse he grew, until, as a last hope, the father went in great haste for Jesus.

When the nobleman told what he had come for, Jesus said to him, "Except ye see signs and wonders, ye will not believe."

The man, in his distress, cried out, "Sir, come down, ere my child die." And Jesus said to him, "Go thy way; thy son liveth."

Without a word, the nobleman started for home. His son was far away, but the father believed that Jesus had made him well.

And as the nobleman believed, so it was. The fever left the son at the very time when Jesus said, "Go thy way; thy son liveth."

From that time, the nobleman and all that were in his house believed that Jesus was the Christ, the Son of God.

Nobleman	nigh	last	signs	fever
wonders	near	worse	hope	heard
about	grew	haste	without	healed
wonderful	doing	until	except	distress

TEACHING HUMILITY.

Jesus walked from place to place, all the time healing the sick and teaching the people. As they heard of the things he did and the words he spoke, they came from every way to see and hear so wonderful a man.

Sometimes the people were so many that he had to have them stand on the shore of the lake, while he went out a little way and taught them from a boat.

It is likely that the boat was in a place where the water makes up into land, and the land comes around on each side so far that the people at the ends would be about as near to Jesus as those in the middle of the company. In this way they could all hear him and see him, but could not crowd upon him.

At one time he went up into a little mountain in sight of a beautiful lake. The people came in great numbers, and Jesus stood above them, and talked to them a long time.

He told them many things that they had never been taught before. They had always thought that the rich and the proud were the happy ones.

Jesus taught that humble people, who love God and men, and who do not care for praise, are the ones who are blessed and happy. He said, "Blessed are the poor in spirit; for theirs is the kingdom of heaven."

The poor in spirit are humble. They do not think too highly of themselves. They do not think that they are better than other people. They are sorry for their sins,—sorry that they do not love God more. They know that they are poor and needy,—that they are lost without a Saviour. They will come to Christ, and he will lead them into his kingdom.

Teaching	lake	stood	humble	think
spoke	little	before	blessed	themselves
stand	boat	rich	kingdom	highly
shore	numbers	proud	poor	lead

WHO ARE HAPPY.

"Blessed are they that mourn; for they shall be comforted."

If we mourn for our sins, we may be forgiven. If we mourn for friends, God can give us others. If we mourn for losses, God may give us something better. If we mourn for the evil that is in the earth, we may still be comforted; for this will all come to an end.

God's Holy Spirit is the great Comforter, and God is always willing to give it. There is no sorrow that the Spirit cannot soothe.

"Blessed are the meek; for they shall inherit the earth."

Yes; they will live on the earth after the proud are all destroyed. If all men were meek, there would be no strife, and no war. No one would be trying to get the highest place.

Moses was the meekest man on earth. He was not willing to be the leader of God's people.

If all who believed on Jesus had been meek, they would not have been talking about who should be greatest in his kingdom.

Jesus knew how much all men need the lessons that he was teaching.

Mourn	losses	inherit	war	needed
evil	trying	lessons	still	comforted
meek	highest	forgiven	soothe	destroyed
friends	Moses	teaching	strife	Comforter

MERCY, PURITY, AND PEACE.

"Blessed are the merciful: for they shall obtain mercy."

It is easy to forgive those we love. God loves all men. So should we. Then we can forgive all, and delight to show them mercy.

If we forgive not others, how can we hope to be forgiven? We must love as God loves. Then we have the spirit of forgiveness.

"Blessed are the pure in heart: for they shall see God."

It is love that makes the heart pure. "Love thinketh no evil." All bad deeds come from bad thoughts. From pure thoughts come deeds of mercy and love.

The pure in heart will see God in heaven. They will also see him in his works on earth, — in the sky and the sea, the trees and the grass, the birds and the flowers, — in rocks, streams, mountains, and valleys. And everywhere they will see that "God is love."

"Blessed are the peacemakers: for they shall be called the children of God."

God is called a God of peace. Christ is called the Prince of peace. To be a peacemaker, then, is to be like God and Christ. To be like them is to be a child of God. And I may be a child of God, — may be one of God's family on earth, as well as in heaven!

"The wisdom that is from above is first pure, then peaceable." Christ's gospel is called the gospel of peace. Love and peace are among the fruits of the Spirit. If the Spirit of God is in us, we shall be peacemakers.

Hope	called	merciful	grass	prince
sea	obtain	forgiveness	streams	valleys
sky	heart	peaceable	wisdom	delight
fruits	mercy	peacemakers	deeds	family

LOVE TO ENEMIES.

Jesus taught that we should not love our friends only, but our enemies also. That we should pray for them, no matter how badly they may use us.

Some thought this a hard thing to do. But Jesus said, "If ye love them which love you, what thank have ye? for sinners also love those that love them.

"And if ye do good to them which do good to you, what thank have ye? for sinners also do even the same."

"But love ye your enemies, and do good, and lend, hoping for nothing again; and your reward shall be great, and ye shall be the children of the Highest: for he is kind unto the unthankful and to the evil.

"Be ye therefore merciful, as your Father also is merciful."

It is not easy to love our enemies, till God puts his love into our hearts. Then we cannot help loving them, and it makes us happy to do so.

And Jesus also said, "Judge not, and ye shall not be judged: condemn not, and ye shall not be condemned: forgive, and ye shall be forgiven.

"Give, and it shall be given unto you; good measure, pressed down, and shaken together, and running over, shall men give into your bosom.

"For with the same measure that ye mete withal it shall be measured to you again."

Enemies	lend	measure	running	matter
therefore	help	nothing	pressed	bosom
unthankful	judge	which	reward	shaken
condemn	again	withal	together	thank

THE NEW COMMANDMENT.

"A new commandment I give unto you, That ye love one another; as I have loved you, that ye also love one another. By this shall all men know that ye are my disciples, if ye have love one to another." John 13:34, 35.

"Beloved, let us love one another: for love is of God; and every one that loveth is born of God, and knoweth God. He that loveth not, knoweth not God; for God is love.

"In this was manifested the love of God toward us, because that God sent his only begotten Son into the world, that we might live through him." "Beloved, if God so loved us, we ought also to love one another."

"We know that we have passed from death

unto life, because we love the brethren. He that loveth not his brother abideth in death."

"Hereby perceive we the love of God, because he laid down his life for us: and we ought to lay down our lives for the brethren.

"But whoso hath this world's good, and seeth his brother have need, and shutteth up his bowels of compassion from him, how dwelleth the love of God in him?

"My little children, let us not love in word, neither in tongue; but in deed and in truth."

"There is no fear in love; but perfect love casteth out fear. . . . He that feareth is not made perfect in love." "And this commandment have we of him, That he who loveth God love his brother also." 1 John 4:18, 21.

We have this commandment also,—"That we should believe on the name of his Son Jesus Christ, and love one another."

Love is the first fruit of the Spirit; and if we have not love, we have not the Spirit of God, and are not his children. Faith is the fruit of the Spirit, and works by love.

Commandment	disciples	begotten	abideth
manifested	dwelleth	shutteth	bowels
compassion	brethren	perceive	neither
because	beloved	tongue	perfect
casteth	toward	name	serve

THE EARTH AT CREATION.

Creation.

TEXT.— "In the beginning God created the heaven and the earth." Genesis 1 : 1.

OUR God is a great God. His ways are past finding out. He made all things; and Christ our Saviour was with his Father in all his wonderful work.

So we read of Christ in God's holy book, that " all things were made by him; and without him was not anything made that was made."

God and Christ are one. They have the same mind. They do the same work. They work together now. They worked together in making the worlds.

God made this earth where we now live. It seems strange to think there was a time, thousands of years ago, when this earth was nowhere to be found; but so it was.

When men make things, they have to have tools to work with. They have to make things little by little, working at them a long time before they are done.

It was not so with God when he made this earth. " He spake, and it was done. He commanded, and it stood fast."

At first, the earth was covered with water, and darkness rested upon it everywhere. Nothing could live on it as it was then. So God went to work to make it a beautiful and happy home for man.

On the FIRST day the Lord made light. "And God called the light Day, and the darkness he called Night."

On the SECOND day he made the air we breathe, and in which the birds fly.

On the THIRD day he made the land, seas, and rivers, and the grass, flowers, and trees.

On the FOURTH day he made the sun, moon, and stars, to give light to the earth by day and night.

On the FIFTH day he made the fish that swim in the water, and the birds that fly in the air.

On the SIXTH day he made man and all the animals that live on the land. And he gave them for food the grain of the fields, the fruit of the trees, and the vegetables of the garden.

On the SEVENTH day God rested "from all the work which he had made." "And God saw everything that he had made, and, behold, it was very good."

God created the earth, and everything that lives and grows on it, in six days. He rested the Seventh day, and looked over the work he had finished. Then he blessed it and made it his holy Sabbath.

When the Sabbath comes, he wants us to stop our work and play, and look at the beautiful things that are around us, and remember that he made them for us.

And when we are in danger of forgetting the Sabbath, let us read Exodus 20:8-11, which tells us when and why he made it.

The Confusion of Tongues.

TEXT.— "Let us build us a city, and a tower whose top may reach unto heaven; and let us make us a name." Genesis 11:4.

FOR more than two thousand years there was but one language on the earth. No matter where one might go, he found the people telling their thoughts in the same words.

Once the people had gone so far from God and his ways, that a great flood of water rolled over the earth and drowned them nearly all.

Noah was a good man; and God saved him and his family in the ark. God told Noah what was going to happen, and showed him how to build the ark.

For years, Noah warned the people that if they did not leave their bad ways and turn to God, they would be swept away and drowned by a flood. But they would not believe his words, and went on from bad to worse.

After the flood, there were only eight persons left alive,— four men and four women. But in course of time these eight had become a multitude.

Little by little they had forgotten the good teachings of Noah. They took their own way, and so grew proud and wicked.

They wanted to make themselves a great name; and so they planned to build a mighty tower, that, as they said, should reach unto heaven.

THE TOWER OF BABEL.

They chose a beautiful plain by the side of a river, in the land of Shinar, and there they went to making bricks for a city and a tower.

They builded and builded; and year by year the tower grew higher, and the city grew larger. In this way the work went on for a long time.

At last, God thought the time had come to check their pride. So he sent his angels to confuse their speech. All at once they found that they could not understand one another. When the men who had charge of the work gave orders, no one could make out what they wanted.

Of course the work could not go on in this way, and it had to be given up. From that time to this, there have been different languages in the world, and the people of one country cannot understand the speech of those who belong to other countries.

These people knew that they were not living as God would have them live. They knew that they were selfish, and proud, and wicked, and were afraid that God might destroy them as he destroyed the people before the flood.

How foolish it was of them to think that they could save themselves by building a tower so high that the waters of a flood could not cover it!

By trying to do this, they showed that they did not believe God; for he had promised never to destroy the earth by a flood again. So it is that foolishness and unbelief go together.

The Favorite Son.

TEXT.— "Now Israel loved Joseph more than all his children, because he was the son of his old age; and he made him a coat of many colors." Genesis 37:3.

NOAH was a man chosen of God to teach the truth to the world. He lived after the flood three hundred and fifty years. He was alive when the tower and city of Babel were building, and many, many years after.

Now God always has some one on the earth to bear witness to the truth,— to teach people how to live happily here, and gain a home in heaven hereafter. So after Noah died, the Lord raised up another man to bear the light of love and truth to the world.

Two years after the death of Noah, Abraham was born. As he grew to be a man, the Lord gave him much wisdom. He also was faithful in all things. The Lord could trust him to do just as he told him to do.

To Abraham, the Lord showed things that were to come to pass many years afterward. He made him precious promises. He said he would bless him, and bless his children, his children's children, and so on, till at last Christ, the Saviour of the world, should come in the line of his family.

Abraham had a dear son, called Isaac, who was faithful, like his father. He was so good a man that the Bible says nothing against him. Now Isaac had two sons; but they could not agree, and one of them, Jacob, had to go far from home and stay there many years. When he came back, he had twelve sons.

These sons had different mothers, and did not always agree so well as brothers should. As they came to be men, they were often unkind to their father, and took their own way instead of obeying him. The more they did wrong, the more hard-hearted they grew to be.

But the two younger sons, Joseph and Benjamin, had a kinder nature. They loved their father, and felt sorry when their older brothers were rude to him.

Joseph had a remarkable mind, and while he was quite a lad, the Lord gave him dreams that seemed to show that he was to be a great man.

The Lord had chosen him for a great work, not because he was partial to Joseph, but because he knew that he would be faithful and true.

Jacob loved Joseph because he was a son of his old age and of his beloved wife Rachel. He also loved him because he was so kind and obedient.

But the more that Jacob loved Joseph, the more his brothers hated him; for they were very jealous. But when he told his dreams, their hatred became so great that some of them wanted to kill him. And they said to him, "Shalt thou indeed reign over us?"

Even his father could hardly have faith in his second dream, where he saw the sun, moon, and stars

THE SELLING OF JOSEPH.

bow down to him. He said to Joseph, "Shall I and thy mother and thy brethren indeed come to bow down ourselves to thee to the earth?"

They looked upon Joseph as but a boy, and could not see why the Lord had chosen him, instead of his older brothers, who were some of them powerful men. But the Lord sees not as man sees. He can look into the heart and understand all its workings.

Jacob and his sons had many cattle, and they had to be watched, and taken from one part of the country to another to find grass; for the fields were not fenced off into pastures.

At one time Jacob had not heard from his sons for a number of days, and so he sent Joseph to look them up, and bring him word how they were. When they saw him coming, they said to one another, "Behold, this dreamer cometh;" and they laid plans to kill him.

At first they cast him into a pit, but afterward they took him out, and sold him to some merchantmen who were going to Egypt.

Then they dipped his coat in the blood of a kid, and took it to his father, saying, "This have we found: know now whether it be thy son's coat or no.

"And he knew it, and said, It is my son's coat; an evil beast hath devoured him; Joseph is without doubt rent in pieces. And Jacob rent his clothes, and put sackcloth upon his loins, and mourned for his son many days."

Joseph Interpreting Pharaoh's Dream.

Faithfulness Rewarded.

TEXT.—"But the Lord was with Joseph, and showed him mercy, and gave him favor in the sight of the keeper of the prison." Genesis 39:21.

NOW the men who bought Joseph of his brethren, sold him in Egypt to Potiphar, the captain of the king's guard. "And his master saw that the Lord was with him, and that the Lord made all that he did to prosper in his hand."

So Potiphar made Joseph overseer of his house, and put all he had into Joseph's hands to be cared for. And the Lord blessed Potiphar's house for Joseph's sake. "And the blessing of the Lord was upon all that he had in the house, and in the field."

But Potiphar's wife told a wicked lie about Joseph, and so got him put in prison. Yet the Lord blessed Joseph, even there. The keeper of the prison, seeing how just and wise he was, let him go freely about the prison, helping to take care of the other prisoners.

Now there were two of the king's officers in the prison, and they were troubled about some dreams they had had. And Joseph said, Tell them to me; perhaps the Lord will show me their meaning.

When they had told their dreams, Joseph said that the king was going to hang one of the men, and set the other one free. And it happened just as Joseph had said.

Two years after this, the king had a strange dream, and none of the wise men of his kingdom could tell its meaning. Now the king's chief butler, the man who had been in prison with Joseph, and had been set free, told the king about Joseph.

When Joseph had been sent for, and brought before the king, he told the king that it was the Lord who had given him his dream, and that it was the Lord who would show its meaning.

He said there were to be seven years of plenty, and then seven years of famine. In the first seven years the land would bring forth grain abundantly, and a part of it must be laid by for the seven years of famine; for in those years nothing would grow.

So the king set Joseph as first ruler over all the land of Egypt, and had him store up the corn for seven years.

"And Pharaoh took off his ring from his hand, and put it upon Joseph's hand, and arrayed him in vestures of fine linen, and put a gold chain about his neck; and he made him to ride in the second chariot which he had; and they cried before him, Bow the knee: and he made him ruler over all the land of Egypt."

When the famine came on, it was in other countries, as well as in Egypt, and Joseph's ten brothers came to Egypt to buy corn. Now every one who bought corn had to come to Joseph. When his brothers came, he knew them, but they knew not him.

So he acted as though they were enemies, and put them in prison as spies. How they must have felt! Their wives and children were at home with very little food, and no one to get them any more.

These cruel brothers began to think that God was going to punish them for their sin in selling Joseph. They said, "We are verily guilty concerning our brother; . . . therefore is this distress come upon us."

But Joseph was sorry for them, and felt afraid that those they had left behind might suffer. So after he had kept them in ward three days, he set them all free but one, gave them as much corn as they could carry, and started them on their way home.

One of them he kept till they should bring down Benjamin, to prove that they had told him the truth; for he had questioned them very closely about their family.

So they went with their corn, and when it was nearly eaten up, Jacob wanted them to go to Egypt for more; but they said it would be of no use to go without Benjamin; for the man had told them plainly that they could not see his face again unless they brought their younger brother with them.

Then Jacob was in great distress. Joseph was not, Simeon was a prisoner in Egypt, and now he was afraid of losing Benjamin, his youngest. But at last he gave his consent, and they went on their way, taking with them money for their corn, and a present for Joseph.

Joseph's Dream.

Joseph's Dream Fulfilled.

TEXT.—And Judah and his brethren came to Joseph's house; for he was yet there; and they fell before him on the ground." Genesis 44:14.

AND when Joseph saw Benjamin with them, he said to the ruler of his house, Bring these men home, and slay, and make ready; for these men shall dine with me at noon."

But the brothers were afraid to be brought into Joseph's house. They had been accused of being spies when they came there before, and thought it likely that something would be brought against them now.

Now the money they paid for corn when they came there the first time, had been put back into their corn sacks with the corn, and they were afraid they might be charged with stealing it.

So they told the steward of Joseph's house that they had brought that money back, besides money enough to buy more corn. And the man said, " Peace be to you, fear not; your God, and the God of your father, hath given you treasure in your sacks: I had your money. And he brought Simeon out unto them."

"And when Joseph came home, they brought him the present which was in their hand into the house, and bowed themselves to him to the earth. And he asked them of their welfare, and said, Is your father well, the old man of whom ye spake? Is he yet alive?"

"And he lifted up his eyes, and saw his brother Benjamin, his mother's son, and said, Is this your younger brother, of whom ye spake unto me? and he said, God be gracious unto thee, my son."

Then he went away from them, and shut himself up in his own chamber and wept. But afterward he washed his face, and came out to them, and treated them kindly. A great dinner was prepared for them, and Joseph himself went in, and waited on them.

"And he commanded the steward of his house, saying, Fill the men's sacks with food, as much as they can carry, and put every man's money in his sack's mouth.

"And put my cup, the silver cup, in the sack's mouth of the youngest, and his corn money. And he did according to the word that Joseph had spoken.

"As soon as the morning was light, the men were sent away, they and their asses. And when they were gone out of the city, and not yet far off, Joseph said unto his steward, Up, follow after the men; and when thou dost overtake them, say unto them: —

"Wherefore have ye rewarded evil for good? Is not this it in which my lord drinketh, and whereby indeed he divineth? Ye have done evil in so doing. And he overtook them, and he spake unto them these same words."

They told him that they knew nothing about the cup. They would not steal, especially from one who had been so kind to them. If they were not honest men, they would not have brought back the money they found in their sacks when they got home from their first journey.

Finally, they told him to search, and see if they had stolen anything. They said that if he found that any of them had stolen the cup, the one who had done the deed should die, and all the rest of them would be Joseph's bond servants.

Then every man's sack was searched, and in Benjamin's sack they found the cup, just where it had been put; but Benjamin did not know it was there. "Then they rent their clothes, and laded every man his ass, and returned to the city.

"And Judah and his brethren came to Joseph's house; for he was yet there; and they fell before him on the ground. And Joseph said unto them, What deed is this that ye have done? wot ye not that such a man as I can certainly divine?

"And Judah said, What shall we say unto my lord? What shall we speak? or how shall we clear ourselves? God hath found out the iniquity of thy servants. Behold, we are my lord's servants, both we, and he also with whom the cup is found."

Joseph would not consent to this. He would keep only the one in whose sack the cup had been found. The others must hurry home with their corn.

JACOB GOING DOWN TO EGYPT.

Brotherly Love Restored.

"TEXT.— "Moreover he kissed all his brethren, and wept upon them; and after that his brethren talked with him." Genesis 45 : 15.

THEN Judah stepped up close to Joseph, and said, "O my lord, let thy servant, I pray thee, speak a word in my lord's ears, and let not thine anger burn against thy servant; for thou art even as Pharaoh.

"My lord asked his servants, saying, Have ye a father, or a brother? And we said unto my lord, We have a father, an old man, and a child of his old age, a little one; and his brother is dead, and he alone is left of his mother, and his father loveth him.

"And thou saidst unto thy servants, Bring him down unto me, that I may set mine eyes upon him. And we said unto my lord, The lad cannot leave his father; for if he should leave his father, his father would die.

"And thou saidst unto thy servants, Except your youngest brother come down with you, ye shall see my face no more. And it came to pass when we came up unto thy servant my father, we told him the words of my lord.

"And our father said, Go again, and buy us a little food. And we said, We cannot go down; if our youngest brother be with us, then will we go down; for we may not see the man's face, except our youngest brother be with us.

"And thy servant my father said unto us, Ye know that my wife bare me two sons; and the one went out from me, and I said, surely he is torn in pieces; and I saw him not since; and if ye take this also from me, and mischief befall him, ye shall bring down my gray hairs with sorrow to the grave.

"Now therefore when I come to thy servant my father, and the lad be not with us, seeing that his life is bound up in the lad's life; it shall come to pass, when he seeth that the lad is not with us, that he will die; and thy servant shall bring down the gray hairs of thy servant our father with sorrow to the grave.

"For thy servant became surety for the lad unto my father, saying, If I bring him not unto thee, then I shall bear the blame to my father forever.

"Now therefore, I pray thee, let thy servant abide instead of the lad a bondman to my Lord; and let the lad go up with his brethren.

"For how shall I go up to my father, and the lad be not with me? lest peradventure I see the evil that shall come on my father.

"Then Joseph could not refrain himself before all them that stood by him; and he cried, Cause every man to go out from me. And there stood no man with him, while Joseph made himself known unto his brethren.

"And he wept aloud; and the Egyptians and the house of Pharaoh heard. And Joseph said unto his brethren, I am Joseph; doth my father yet live? And his brethren could not answer him; for they were troubled at his presence."

But Joseph had forgiven them for all the wrong they had done him. His heart yearned toward them with a brother's love; and he said, "Come near to me, I pray you. And they came near. And he said, I am Joseph your brother, whom ye sold into Egypt.

"Now therefore be not grieved, nor angry with yourselves, that ye sold me hither; for God did send me before you to preserve life."

He told them that God had made him a father to Pharaoh and lord over his house. He had also made him ruler over Egypt, and given him power to save up the corn, so that the family that God had chosen should be kept alive. He said: —

"Haste ye, and go up to my father, and say unto him, Thus saith thy son Joseph, God hath made me lord of all Egypt; come down unto me, tarry not.

"And thou shalt dwell in the land of Goshen, and thou shalt be near unto me, thou, and thy children, and thy children's children; and thy flocks, and thy herds, and all that thou hast; and there will I nourish thee; for yet there are five years of famine."

After this, "he fell upon his brother Benjamin's neck, and wept; and Benjamin wept upon his neck. Moreover he kissed all his brethren, and wept upon them; and after that his brethren talked with him."

When Pharaoh, the king, heard that these men were Joseph's brothers, he was very kind to them, and sent wagons to bring their father, their wives, and their children to Egypt.

At first, Jacob could not believe the good news that Joseph was living; but when they told him all that Joseph had said, and he saw the wagons that Joseph had sent, he said, "It is enough; Joseph my son is yet alive; I will go and see him before I die."

The Lord appeared to Jacob in a vision, and told him not to be afraid to go to Egypt to live; for he would make of him a great nation there, and in time would bring them back to Canaan, as he had promised Abraham.

So they went into Egypt, seventy persons. About two hundred years afterward, when they went up out of that land, they were more than six hundred thousand men, besides women and children.

But in these two hundred years many hard trials came upon the children of Israel. While Joseph lived, all went well with them. After that, there was a new king, who did not care for what Joseph had done, and was not friendly to the Israelites.

He made slaves of them, and they had to work very hard. He kept on making their work harder and harder till it was more than they could do, no matter how hard they tried. Then he ordered that all the male children should be drowned in the river.

But the same God that cared for Joseph remembered them, and in due time raised up Moses, a great leader, and set them free.

Water from the Rock.

TEXT.— "And thou shalt smite the rock, and there shall come water out of it, that the people may drink." Exodus 17:6.

IT was a weary journey,— that journey from Egypt to Canaan, with that vast multitude of people, their children, their cattle, and such earthly goods as they could carry.

There were many dangers to meet on the way; but God had promised to go before them, and prepare a way for them.

At Rephidim there was no water. Without waiting to see what the Lord would do, the angry people cried out to Moses, "Give us water, that we may drink."

They seemed to think it was Moses who was providing for them. This was wrong. Moses could not do any miracles unless the Lord should direct him. So Moses said, "Why chide ye with me? wherefore do ye tempt the Lord?"

At last they grew very bitter, and said to Moses, "Wherefore is this, that thou hast brought us up out of Egypt, to kill us and our children and our cattle with thirst?"

These people had been slaves in Egypt for many years, and had suffered things that were hard to bear. The Lord had sent Moses to get them away from the cruel treatment of a wicked king. And now they

BRINGING WATER FROM THE ROCK.

accused him of bringing them out into that desert place to kill them and their children.

Moses loved these people with a great love,— almost as God himself loved them,— and he was in great distress when he heard them talk as they did. He felt more sorry for them than for himself; for he knew that they were committing a great sin.

He had nowhere else to go; so he cried to the Lord, saying, "What shall I do unto this people? they be almost ready to stone me.

"And the Lord said unto Moses, Go on before the people, and take with thee of the elders of Israel; and thy rod, wherewith thou smotest the river, take in thine hand, and go.

"Behold, I will stand before thee there upon the rock in Horeb; and thou shalt smite the rock, and there shall come water out of it, that the people may drink. And Moses did so in the sight of the elders of Israel."

What a sight it must have been to see so great a multitude crowding to the stream to quench their thirst at this water from the rock!

This rock is an emblem of Christ. The water is the "water of life," that he will give to all who thirst for it. It is the well-spring of love, faith, and hope.

"Ho, every one that thirsteth, come ye to the waters." "If any man thirst, let him come unto me, and drink." "And whosoever will, let him take the water of life freely."

Israelites Gathering Manna.

[64]

Bread from Heaven.

TEXT.— "I will rain bread from heaven for you." Exodus 16:4.

WHEN the Israelites left Egypt, they left in great haste. It was on the night of the passover, when each family had killed a lamb, and eaten it with their garments on, staff in hand, and everything ready to start on their journey.

At midnight came the cry that the first-born had died in every house of the Egyptians. Then the Egyptians hurried Moses and his people out of the land. They would not let the Israelites stay till morning; for, said they, "We be all dead men."

There was not time to raise and bake bread for the journey; so they took dough in their kneading dishes, wrapped it in some of their clothes, and carried it on their shoulders. This dough they must have baked in a very rude way, at night, as they journeyed.

This bread could not have tasted very well; but it was better than none; and when it was all gone, they knew not what to do. At last, when they had been journeying about a month, they thought they should starve if they had to go without bread any longer.

So they began to cry out all over the camp that Moses and Aaron had brought them out there into that barren country to kill them with hunger. They thought more of having something good to eat, than they did of getting free from the cruel Egyptians, or of pleasing the Lord, who was leading them out.

In their distress they said, "Would to God we had died by the hand of the Lord in the land of Egypt, when we sat by the flesh pots, and when we did eat bread to the full."

"And the Lord spake unto Moses, saying, I have heard the murmurings of the children of Israel: speak unto them, saying, At even ye shall eat flesh, and in the morning ye shall be filled with bread; and ye shall know that I am the Lord your God.

"And it came to pass, that at even the quails came up, and covered the camp: and in the morning the dew lay round about the host. And when the dew that lay was gone up, behold, upon the face of the wilderness there lay a small round thing, as small as the hoar frost on the ground."

"And Moses said unto them, This is the bread which the Lord hath given you to eat."

On the morning of the sixth day they were to gather twice as much as on other mornings; and on the morning of the seventh day no manna was to be found.

On other days, if any manna was left over, it spoiled, but on the seventh day it kept good. In this way the Lord marked the true seventh-day Sabbath, that he had sanctified at the creation.

Elijah and the Priests of Baal.

TEXT.— "How long halt ye between two opinions? if the Lord be God, follow him: but if Baal, then follow him." 1 Kings 18:21.

AT one time there was a wicked king in Israel by the name of Ahab. Most of the people followed the ways of king Ahab; and the worship of idols became more common than the worship of God.

So Elijah, the prophet of the Lord, said to Ahab, "As the Lord God of Israel liveth, before whom I stand, there shall not be dew nor rain these years, but according to my word."

For three years and a half there was no rain in Israel. Ahab was very angry that the Lord hid Elijah for the greater part of this time.

Finally, Elijah told Ahab to gather all the prophets of Baal together on Mount Carmel.

"And Elijah came unto all the people, and said, How long halt ye between two opinions? if the Lord be God, follow him; but if Baal, then follow him. And the people answered him not a word.

"Then said Elijah unto the people, I, even I only, remain a prophet of the Lord; but Baal's prophets are four hundred and fifty men.

"Let them therefore give us two bullocks; and let them choose one bullock for themselves, and cut it

ELIJAH'S OFFERING.

in pieces, and lay it on wood, and put no fire under: and I will dress the other bullock, and lay it on wood, and put no fire under:

"And call ye on the name of your gods, and I will call on the name of the Lord: and the God that answereth by fire, let him be God. And all the people answered and said, It is well spoken."

So the prophets of Baal chose their bullock, and did with him as Elijah had said. Then they called upon the name of Baal from morning till noon, saying, "O Baal, hear us!" But no voice answered.

Then they leaped upon the altar, and cut themselves with knives till the blood gushed out upon them. In this way they went on till nearly night, but no fire kindled on the altar.

Then Elijah built an altar of twelve great stones, and laid the wood and the bullock upon it. When all was ready, he had the people pour twelve barrels of water on the altar; so that the wood was drenched, and the trench around the altar was filled with water.

Then Elijah called on the name of the Lord, saying, "Hear me, O Lord, hear me, that this people may know that thou art the Lord God."

"Then the fire of the Lord fell, and consumed the burnt sacrifice, and the wood, and the stones, and the dust, and licked up the water that was in the trench.

"And when all the people saw it, they fell on their faces: and they said, The Lord, he is the God; the Lord, he is the God."

HANDWRITING ON THE WALL.

The Handwriting on the Wall.

TEXT.—"In the same hour came forth fingers of a man's hand, and wrote . . . . upon the plaster of the wall of the king's palace." Daniel 5:5.

BELSHAZZAR, king of Babylon, made a feast, and invited all the great men of his kingdom to come to it.

They ate and drank in great glee, and when the king's head was turned with wine, he commanded to bring in the holy vessels which had been stolen from the temple at Jerusalem.

Now these vessels had been made holy to the Lord, and were not to be used, except by the priests in the temple.

Belshazzar knew this very well, but he had become proud, and meant to show contempt to the God of heaven. So he, and his lords, and his wives drank wine out of these vessels.

But in the midst of their joy, there appeared the fingers of a man's hand, writing something on the wall in front of the king. The king saw the part of the hand that wrote, and began to shake with fear.

He called in all his wise men, but none of them could read the writing or tell its meaning. Just then the queen came in, and by her advice Belshazzar sent for Daniel, who had been brought from Jerusalem by the king's grandfather.

Daniel promised to read the writing, but before beginning to read, he told how God had taught the king's grandfather to be humble, and to know that the most high God can rule the kingdoms of this earth, and give them to whom he will. Then he said,—

"And thou his son, O Belshazzar, hast not humbled thine heart, though thou knewest all this; but hast lifted up thyself against the Lord of heaven; and they have brought the vessels of his house before thee, and thou, and thy lords, thy wives, and thy concubines, have drunk wine in them;

"And thou hast praised the gods of silver, and gold, of brass, iron, wood, and stone, which see not, nor hear, nor know: and the God in whose hand thy breath is, and whose are all thy ways, hast thou not glorified: then was the part of the hand sent from him; and this writing was written."

Then Daniel read the writing, and told what it meant. It was in three parts, and this is the meaning:—

"God hath numbered thy kingdom, and finished it."

"Thou art weighed in the balances, and art found wanting."

"Thy kingdom is divided and given to the Medes and Persians."

The king had little time to repent; for, "In that night was Belshazzar the king of the Chaldeans slain. And Darius the Median took the kingdom."

The Three Hebrews and the Fiery Furnace.

TEXT.—"Be it known unto thee, O king, that we will not serve thy gods, nor worship the golden image which thou hast set up." Daniel 3:18.

WHEN Daniel was taken as a prisoner to Babylon, there were taken with him three others, who were his special friends. These men loved the Lord so well, and served him so truly, that it was safe to give them great wisdom. And the king of Babylon, seeing how wise they were, made them rulers in his kingdom, and gave them new names.

The king and people of Babylon did not serve the true God, but made images, and worshiped them. Could such gods help one in trouble? Could they forgive sins, and make the heart pure? But the king wanted to show his power; and so he made a great image of gold, almost a hundred feet high, and then set a day when all his rulers and captains must come and worship it.

When the day came, the king had a band of music ready, near the image, and not far off was a great fiery furnace. Then his herald cried with a loud voice, and told all the people who had come together at the king's command, that when they heard the band of music begin to play, they must all fall down and worship the image. And if they did not do so, they were to be thrown into the furnace of fire, and burned to death.

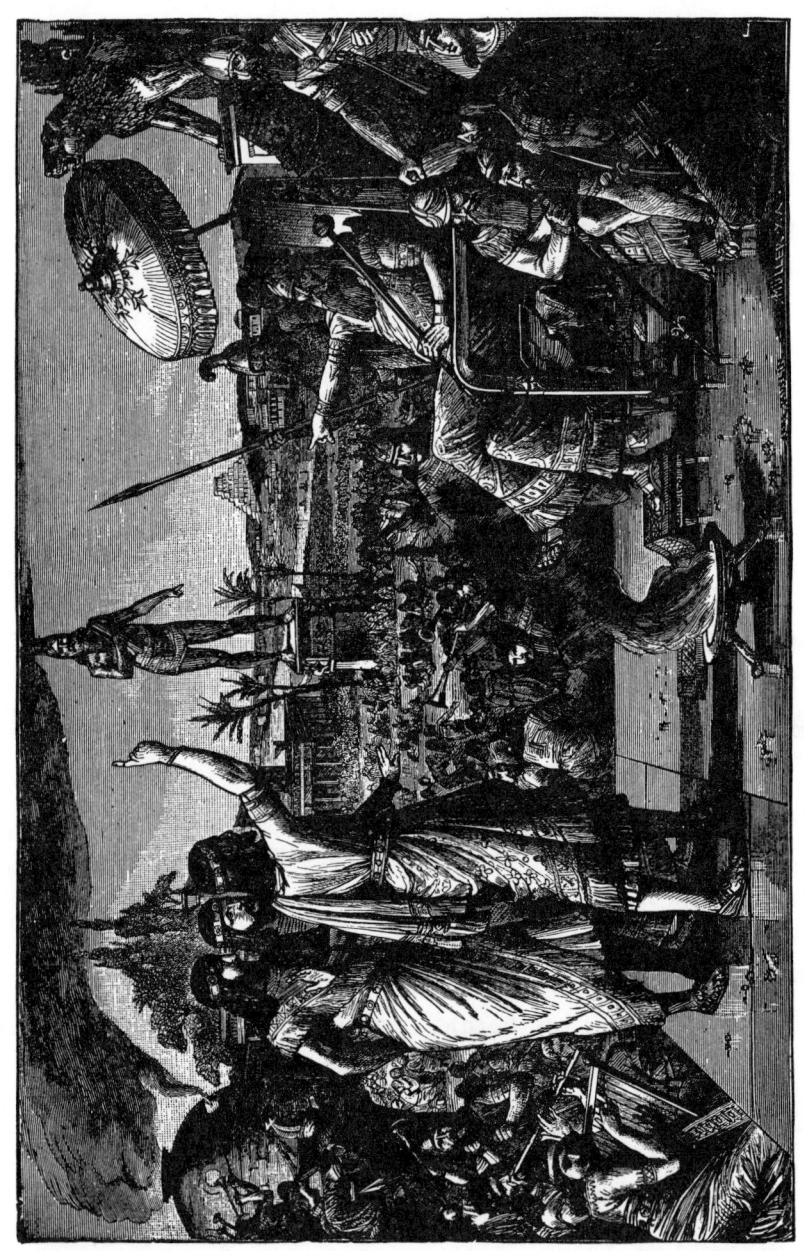

The Three Hebrews before the King.

When all the people had come together, the king commanded the band to play; and when the people heard it, they fell down and worshiped the image. But God had said that men must not worship any image, nor any god but the God who made the earth, and whose home is in heaven. If you would like to read where he says this in the Bible, you will find it in Exodus 20:4, 5.

Now Daniel's three friends could not disobey their God by worshiping this image, no matter who might order it. They would rather die than turn against the God of heaven.

Now there were some among the king's great men who hated all Jews, and Daniel's three friends more than others because the king had such respect for their wisdom, and had given them a high place in his kingdom.

So they came to the king, and told him that there were Jews who would not obey him,— who would not worship the image. Among these Jews were Daniel's three friends, whom the king had set over the affairs of Babylon. Their accusers said, "These men, O king, have not regarded thee: they serve not thy gods, nor worship the golden image which thou hast set up."

When the king heard this, he was angry, and sent for the men who would not obey him. When they had come before him, he said to them,

"Now if ye be ready at what time ye hear the sound of the cornet, flute, harp, sackbut, . . . and all

IN THE FIERY FURNACE.

kinds of music, ye fall down and worship the image which I have made, well; but if ye worship not, ye shall be cast the same hour into the midst of a burning fiery furnace; and who is that God that shall deliver you out of my hands?"

The king thought there could not be a god strong enough to save them from harm in such a place as that. But Daniel's friends knew that the God of heaven could save them if that was the best thing to do. If he did not think it best, they were willing to die.

They did not have to wait to think what to do. They said, "We are not careful to answer thee in this matter. If it be so, our God whom we serve is able to deliver us from the burning fiery furnace, and he will deliver us out of thine hand, O king.

"But if not, be it known unto thee, O king, that we will not serve thy gods, nor worship the golden image which thou hast set up."

Then the king was full of fury, and told his men to heat the furnace seven times hotter than it was wont to be heated. When this had been done, the most mighty men of the king's army were called upon to cast these three peace-loving men into the furnace.

They did their work, but it was the last they ever did; for the fire was so hot that it burned them to death.

As the king was looking into the furnace, he was much troubled, and rose up in haste, and said, "Did not we cast three men bound into the midst of the fire?" And they said, "True, O king.

"He answered and said, Lo, I see four men loose, walking in the midst of the fire, and they have no hurt; and the form of the fourth is like the Son of God."

Then the king went as near as he could to the mouth of the furnace, and said, "Ye servants of the most high God, come forth, and come hither." And they came forth from the midst of the fire.

Then the princes, and all the king's great men, saw these men, "upon whose bodies the fire had no power, nor was an hair of their head singed, neither were their coats changed, nor the smell of fire had passed on them."

Then the king had to own that there is no God like the God that Daniel and his friends worshiped. The people of Babylon thought that Daniel's God was only one among others. The Lord meant to show them that there is but one God, and that he has all power to make or destroy.

Now there were present at that time men from many countries, who would go home, and tell what they had seen; and in that way many people would learn about the God who rules over all.

But if Daniel's three friends had not been true, if they had been afraid to displease the king, and had tried to save their lives by bowing down to the image of gold, then we would not have had this wonderful story to tell.

The Birth of Jesus.

TEXT.— "Behold, I bring you good tidings of great joy, which shall be to all people. For unto you is born this day in the city of David a Saviour, which is Christ the Lord." Luke 2 : 10, 11.

YEARS and years ago, there came to this earth, the most beautiful babe the sun ever shone upon. Mary, his mother, called him Jesus, as God had told her to do.

About this time there were wise men living in the East, hundreds of miles from the place where Jesus was born. These men had studied the Word of God, and learned that it was time for the coming of Emanuel, which means " God with us."

These wise men were not Jews, but they believed in God, and loved him, and praised him as they saw his wonderful works,— the sun, the moon, the stars, and this beautiful earth.

One night, as these men were watching the heavens, they saw a star that they had never seen before. Was this not the sign that they had been looking for? — the star that would lead them to the birthplace of Emanuel.

With joy they went toward the star. But it kept always moving on as they followed.

When they came to Jerusalem, they went to the king, and said, " Where is he that is born king of the Jews; for we have seen his star in the east, and are

THE WISE MEN PRESENTING GIFTS TO JESUS.

[80]

come to worship him." But the king could not tell. He had not been looking for the Saviour, and had not studied the Word of God to see where he was to be born.

So he called all the chief priests and scribes, for these men were supposed to know all about the Scriptures,— and asked them where Christ should be born. And they said, "In Bethlehem of Judea."

Then he talked with the wise men again, and asked them when they first saw the star. He told them to go to Bethlehem, and when they had found the child, to bring him word, that he might go and worship him too.

As they came out from before the king, lo, shining brightly in the sky, was the star that had guided them all the way from the East to Jerusalem. How glad, and how encouraged, they were, when they saw it.

And so, following the star, they came to a place where it stood still, over a stable; and they, wondering much, went in. And what did they see? Why there, cuddled up so cozy and warm, in a manger, lay the babe, with his mother watching beside him.

And were not their hearts filled with joy? Did they not praise God that his promise, made so long ago, was now fulfilled? Yes, indeed. They fell on their knees before the infant Jesus, and worshiped him.

Then they opened their packs, and gave precious gifts of gold, and costly myrrh, and thanked the Lord again and again for the privilege of seeing Jesus.

FLIGHT INTO EGYPT.

Tired with their journey, they sought rest; and that night the Lord gave them a dream, telling them not to go back to Jerusalem, but to go home by another road.

The Lord knew that the king at Jerusalem would try to kill Jesus if he could find him, thinking that he was to be an earthly king, and take king Herod's place. But Jesus was to rule only in the heart, and that by love.

So the wise men went back to their home in the East without seeing the king again. When Herod found out about this, he was angry, and sent his soldiers to kill all the children in Bethlehem under two years of age.

In that way the king thought to kill the infant Jesus; but a power greater than Herod's was guarding this babe; and God told Joseph in a dream to flee to Egypt with the young child and his mother.

And so all the little children of Bethlehem had to die a cruel death by the hand of the rough soldiers; but Jesus was safe with his mother, far on the journey to Egypt.

But by and by Herod died. Then the Lord told Joseph and Mary to go back to the land of Israel. In a dream he showed them that they were to go to Nazareth; and there, in that quiet little town among the hills, Jesus lived and worked till he became a man.

JESUS AMONG THE DOCTORS.

Jesus and the Doctors in the Temple.

TEXT.— "They found him in the temple, sitting in the midst of the doctors, both hearing them and asking them questions." Luke 2:46.

ONCE a year all the people went up to Jerusalem to what was called the feast of the passover. It was not in any sense what we would call a feast now. True, they ate the passover supper; but each family ate by itself, and in the most solemn manner.

This feast was to keep in mind how the Lord had passed over the houses of the Israelites when the first born of every Egyptian family was found dead at midnight.

Each family killed a lamb, and ate it, with loins girded and staff in hand, just as it was done so many years before in Egypt; and the parents were to tell the children what it all meant.

When Jesus was twelve years old, Joseph and Mary took him with them to the feast of the passover. Jesus knew very well that the passover lamb pointed to himself as the Saviour of the world. We can think what his feelings must have been, as he saw the innocent lamb killed and eaten.

When the feast was over, his parents went along with those who were going home by the same road as themselves. They did not see Jesus; but they thought he must be somewhere in the company, and were not anxious about him.

They no doubt found many friends to visit with, and had a pleasant day. But when night came, and Jesus was nowhere to be found, they were much troubled.

The next morning they started on their way back to Jerusalem. The way seemed lonely. They remembered how Herod had tried to take the life of Jesus when he was a little child. They knew that the priests were not friendly, and their hearts ached with fear as they went along.

They began to think how careless they had been. And was their dear son really stolen from them? Had the priests hired robbers to snatch him away, as they went carelessly along? How would they answer to God for being so unfaithful?

But they found no trace of him on the way, and it was not until the third day that they found him in Jerusalem. He was not in any out-of-the-way place, but in the temple, talking with the most learned men of the nation, hearing them, and asking them questions. "And all that heard him were astonished at his understanding and answers.

"And when they saw him, they were amazed; and his mother said unto him, Son, why hast thou thus dealt with us? behold, thy father and I have sought thee sorrowing.

"And he said unto them, How is it that ye sought me? wist ye not that I must be about my Father's business?"

Turning Water into Wine.

TEXT.— "Jesus saith unto them, Fill the waterpots with water. And they filled them up to the brim." John 2 : 7.

JESUS lived in Nazareth till he was about thirty years old. At last the time had come for him to begin his great work of teaching the people.

They had wrong notions; for many of the priests who had been teaching them were selfish men, and did not know the ways of God very well themselves.

Before Jesus began to preach, he went to the river Jordan to be baptized. When he came up out of the water, a dove came down, in sight of all the people, and rested on him. At the same time a voice from heaven said, "This is my beloved Son, in whom I am well pleased."

The dove, an emblem of love, represented the Holy Spirit. It showed that God put his Spirit upon Jesus. It was always with him, and guided him in every thing he did. God is willing to give us the same Spirit to lead us; and while we are led by the Spirit of God, we shall not go wrong.

It was John, who baptized Jesus; and he baptized a great many others besides. He was a man of God, and had been preaching good things to the people. He had been telling them that Christ, the Messiah, would soon appear.

TURNING WATER INTO WINE.

One day, when John saw Jesus coming, he said, "Behold the Lamb of God, which taketh away the sin of the world." Two of John's disciples who heard him say this, went to Jesus and talked with him. Then they went to their friends, and told them that they had found the Christ. To others, Jesus said, "Follow me," and they did so.

In this way a few good men were gathered about Jesus. They believed him to be the Saviour, and followed him everywhere he went. They tried to remember all that he said; and the more they heard, and the longer they were with him, the more sure they were that he was the Christ indeed.

Jesus liked to have these men with him; for he wanted them to learn all they could, so that after his death they might be able to teach to others the same things that he had taught to them.

Afterward, some of these men wrote the life of Jesus, as we have it in the Bible. The Spirit of God helped them, and brought to their minds the things that their dear Lord had said.

Now there was to be a marriage at Cana, a little town not very far from Nazareth. Mary, the mother of Jesus, was asked to be there, and so were Jesus and his disciples. By his disciples we mean those few men who went with him all the time, to listen to his words of wisdom and love.

At the marriage they had a feast; for that was the way people did in those days. And at the feast they had wine. But their wine was not like the wine we have now. It was just the fresh, sweet juice of grapes, and would not make any one drunk.

But before the feast was over, the wine was all gone; and they did not know where to get any more in time for the occasion. Now the man who made the feast was troubled, because he did not want the people who had come to it to know that he had not enough wine for them.

Then the mother of Jesus came to him, and said, "They have no wine." Jesus did not say that he would do anything about it; but Mary said to the servants, "Whatsoever he saith unto you, do it."

Now there were standing there six water-pots of stone. These pots would hold five or six pailfuls apiece. Jesus told the servants to fill them with water; and when they had filled them to the brim, Jesus said, "Draw out now, and bear to the governor of the feast."

What must these servants have thought? for when they began to draw, they found that the water was all turned to wine. And when they took it to the governor, he wondered that the bridegroom had kept the best wine for the last of the feast; for he did not know how the wine had been made.

And when his disciples saw this miracle, they believed on him more fully than before.

The Raising of Jairus' Daughter.

TEXT.—"My little daughter lieth at the point of death; I pray thee, come and lay thy hands on her, that she may be healed." Mark 5:23.

ONE day Jesus was by the Sea of Galilee, at Capernaum. A great many people had heard of his coming, and had come to meet him. Among those who came was a ruler of the synagogue, or Jewish church. The name of this man was Jairus, and he came to beg Jesus to come and see his little daughter, who was very sick. The best doctors had done all they could, and now said they could do no more, and the little girl must die. Jairus was a rich man, and he had spared no money in trying to save the life of his daughter. But we know that we cannot buy life or health with money. God alone can give life.

Jesus was always ready to help all who came to him for help, and he went at once with the sorrowful father. And although it was only a short distance to the home of this ruler, it took a long time to get there, for the people crowded around Jesus, and wanted him to speak to them, and make them well. Among them was a woman who had been sick twelve years, and had spent all her money trying to be made well. She had heard of this wonderful Jesus, and she thought, If I can touch but the hem of his robe, I shall be made well. So she struggled through the crowd that surrounded Jesus, and, stooping down, touched his garment, and,

JESUS RAISING JAIRUS' DAUGHTER.

oh, how wonderful, she felt the healing power of the Saviour coursing through her veins, and she knew that she had been made well.

With gratitude in her heart she tried to get out of the throng, but Jesus stopped, and said, "Who touched me?" All were surprised to hear him ask that question, for he was being pressed on all sides by the eager people who surrounded him. But Jesus said, "Somebody hath touched me; for I perceive that virtue is gone out of me." Jesus could tell whether it was the touch of faith, or of the careless crowd. You can see the people in the picture, crowding around Jesus to be healed.

The woman, seeing that she was found out, came and told Jesus the story of her suffering and belief, and Jesus said, "Daughter, be of good comfort; thy faith hath made thee whole; go in peace." This was to show to the people that it was her faith that had made her whole, and not the mere act of touching his garment.

Jairus had watched closely the working of this miracle, and now felt more sure than ever that Jesus would heal his child. But just then a servant came and said, "Thy daughter is dead." Jesus heard the words which seemed to take away all hope from the sorrowing father, and said to him, "Fear not; believe only, and she shall be made whole." Jairus took fresh hope from this, and they hurried on to his house, and to the room where the dead child was lying. Jesus had

JESUS HEALING THE SICK.

the room cleared of all that were in it, except the parents of the child, and his disciples, " and took her by the hand, and called, saying, Maid, arise." And she arose at once, and was as well and strong as ever. When Jesus came to that house, it was full of weeping and sorrow, but he brought life and joy, and gave the little girl to her father and mother again.

THE SEA OF GALILEE.

[96] JESUS FEEDING THE FIVE THOUSAND.

Jesus Feeds the Five Thousand.

TEXT.— "When Jesus then lifted up his eyes, and saw a great company come unto him, he saith unto Philip, Whence shall we buy bread, that these may eat?" John 6:5.

AND Jesus went across the sea of Galilee into a desert place near Bethsaida. There a great multitude came to him, to hear the wonderful things he always had to say.

Jesus knew how needy these people were; and as he saw them bringing their sick friends to be cured, his great heart of pity went out to them. All day he patiently taught them, healing their sick, and giving them comforting words.

As evening drew on, he looked over that great company, and thought how hungry and tired they must be,— those men and women, and even little children, who had come so far to hear him. If they went off without eating, they might faint by the way.

Jesus did not teach them as they had been taught by the proud priests and Levites. His kind voice was sweet to them, and they were so hungry for his words of life that they forgot their need of other food.

But Jesus remembered them. He did not forget their wants, but asked Philip where bread could be had to feed so many. He did this to try the faith of his disciples; for Jesus himself knew what he would do.

The disciples said, "Send them away, that they may go into the villages, and buy themselves bread." But Jesus said, "Give ye them to eat." Now all the food they had was five loaves and two fishes that a little boy had brought.

Jesus told the disciples to have the people sit down in small companies on the grass. Then he took the food, and looking up to heaven, gave thanks to God for it. In this he set an example for all to follow.

Then he broke the loaves and the fishes, and handed the food to his disciples, and the disciples gave to the people. Jesus kept right on breaking and breaking, and handing out food till all that great multitude had had enough.

Now there were more than five thousand people fed in this way, and all from what a little lad had carried in a basket on his arm. This would make a hundred companies, with fifty persons in each company.

Then Jesus said, "Gather up the fragments, that nothing be lost." Although the food had come to them so abundantly, and without any effort on their part, they were to save every crumb. We should be generous, but never wasteful. What God has in mercy given us, we should never throw away.

The Lord fed these people when they were faint with hunger. He will remember us in all our needs. He clothes the lilies and feeds the sparrows; will he not care for us?

The Fire by the Sea.

TEXT. — "But when the morning was now come, Jesus stood on the shore; but the disciples knew not that it was Jesus." John 21 : 4.

IT was long and long ago that seven sad fishermen toiled all night on the Sea of Galilee, and caught nothing.

They had given up all to follow Jesus, and now he had been taken and crucified. They believed that he had been raised from the dead,— they had even seen him,— but they knew not whether they should see him again, and they were very sorrowful.

He had called them to be fishers of men; but as soon as he was taken from them, they went back to their old work of taking fish from the lake.

But they had no success. So it often is, when men give up the work which God has called them to do.

When the morning broke, they found themselves not far from shore. As they were looking toward the land, they saw a man standing near the edge of the lake. It was Jesus, but they did not know him.

Jesus saw them looking at him, and called out, "Children, have ye any meat?" When they answered "No," he said, "Cast the net on the right side of the ship, and ye shall find.

"They cast therefore, and now they were not able to draw it for the multitude of fishes. Therefore that disciple whom Jesus loved, saith unto Peter, It is the Lord.

The Fire by the Sea.

"Now when Simon Peter heard that it was the Lord, he girt his fisher's coat unto him (for he was naked), and did cast himself into the sea." The other disciples followed in their little boat, "dragging the net with fishes."

"As soon as they were come to land, they saw a fire of coals there, and fish laid thereon, and bread." This showed how easily Jesus could provide for their wants. They thought they were alone and forsaken, but all the time the Saviour was near. He had not lost sight of them.

Jesus did not find fault with them, but said, "Bring of the fish which ye have now caught.

"Simon Peter went up, and drew the net to land full of great fishes, an hundred and fifty and three; and for all there were so many, yet was not the net broken.

"Jesus saith unto them, Come and dine. And none of the disciples durst ask him, Who art thou? knowing that it was the Lord. Jesus then cometh, and taketh bread, and giveth them, and fish likewise.

"This is now the third time that Jesus showed himself to his disciples, after that he was risen from the dead."

It was after this morning meal, by the fire of coals on the beach, that Jesus made Peter answer, three times over, the question, "Lovest thou me?" And three times Peter received the charge, "Feed my sheep."

THE BLIND BEGGAR.

Jesus Heals the Blind Beggar.

TEXT.—"Therefore said they unto him, How were thine eyes opened? He answered and said, A man that is called Jesus made clay, and anointed mine eyes, and said unto me, Go to the pool of Siloam, and wash; and I went and washed, and I received sight." John 9:10, 11.

ONE Sabbath day, after Jesus had been teaching in the Temple, he saw a blind beggar sitting by the side of the street. Jesus was sorry for him, because he could not see the beautiful trees, and the flowers, and the green grass. He had always been blind, and so had never seen his parents and friends.

When Jesus came close to the man, he spat upon the ground, and took some of the dust he had made moist, and put it on the blind eyes, and told the man to go to the pool of Siloam and wash. Jesus could have opened his eyes without sending him to wash in the pool; but he wanted him to show that he believed he would see if he did just as Jesus told him. To believe in Jesus, and trust that he will do just as he has promised, is called faith.

At the bottom of the picture you can see the blind man standing in the pool, washing his eyes. As soon as he had done this his eyes were opened, and he could see as well as you and I can.

When he went home, all by himself, without any one to lead him, his parents and neighbors were very much surprised. In the morning, when he left home, he was blind, and now he could see. Some did not believe it was the blind beggar at all, but thought it was some one who looked like him; "but he said, I am he."

Then they all wanted to know how he had received his sight; and he told them all about it, as you will see by reading the text at the beginning of this story. And when they found out that it was Jesus who had done this wonderful thing, they said to him who had been blind, "Where is he? He said, I know not." You see he was so glad because he could see, that he almost forgot Jesus. Do you ever forget Jesus? He made this beautiful world we live in. And, although we cannot see him, he sees us all the time, and takes care of us. He is ready now to help us, if we will believe in him, and do just as he tells us, as the blind man did.

Jesus did not use any medicine in healing the blind man. Doctors try to cure people now by giving them medicine. Sometimes they get well and sometimes they do not. Jesus healed the sick, and the blind, and the lame, by the power of God. The power of God made man in the first place, and it can heal him when he is sick. All Jesus had to do was to say to the sick, "Be well," and the power of God healed them at once. To heal in this way is called a miracle.

His neighbors were so surprised at this miracle that they took him who had been blind to the Pharisees and Elders of Israel. These men claimed to be good men who understood the Bible and could teach others how to be good. But they were proud, and were really so wicked at heart that they afterward killed Jesus.

These men tried to make the man who was healed believe that Jesus was wicked because he had healed him on the Sabbath. But he believed in him all the more, and said, "If this man were not of God, he could do nothing." Then these Pharisees and Elders were so angry that "they cast him out" of their church and would not let him come there any more.

When Jesus knew that he had been cast out, he went to him and told him that he was the Son of God, the Saviour of the world. "And he said, Lord, I believe. And he worshiped him."

RUINS OF THE POOL OF SILOAM.

JESUS BLESSING LITTLE CHILDREN.

Jesus Blessing Little Children.

TEXT.—"And they brought young children to him, that he should touch them; and his disciples rebuked those that brought them." Mark 10 : 13.

JESUS had a kind face, and all the children liked him. The little ones would stretch out their hands to him and smile at him; for they could see that he had a loving heart.

Jesus loves every one, and whenever he saw any one sick or in trouble, his heart was moved with pity. His heart is as loving and kind now as it was then, and he will as gladly help and bless us, if we will come to him.

If we will let him, he will put into our hearts the same loving spirit. Then we, like him, will love every one. We will visit the sick and the sorrowful, and try to comfort them. This is the work that Jesus has for us to do.

At one time, after Jesus had been teaching the people, some fond mothers brought their little children to him, that he might lay his hands on them and bless them. It was thus that Jacob blessed the two sons of Joseph; and it was still a common thing to lay hands on the heads of those who were prayed for.

When the disciples saw the mothers bringing their children to Jesus, they told them that they ought not to trouble the Master in this way. "But Jesus called them unto him, and said, Suffer little children to come unto me, and forbid them not; for of such is the kingdom of God."

Jesus loves little children. They are innocent and full of trust. We must become like them, if we would please God. Jesus had been a child, and known a mother's love.

He knew how dear these little ones were to their mothers, and would not turn them away. He loves the mothers who live now, as much as he did the mothers who lived then. He is as ready to bless their children. Let the mothers bring them to him.

Do we not wish that we might have been there to see the tender look of the Master as he bent over the sweet young faces?— that we might have heard the tones of his voice, and listened to the words he spoke to those little ones?

But we have many of his words, and can read them over and over again,— read them till we can almost hear how they sounded when they came from his lips. We can talk to him in prayer, and he will give us answers of peace. He will fill our souls with love.

Jesus said, "Except ye be converted, and become as little children, ye shall not enter into the kingdom of heaven." Let us come to Jesus, then, in the simple, undoubting faith of childhood,— come with all the sweet trust that a little child feels toward his mother.

The Sabbath Made for Man.

TEXT.— "Why do ye that which is not lawful to do on the Sabbath days?" Luke 6 : 2.

AT the time when Jesus was upon the earth, the Jews were very strict about keeping the Sabbath. The love of God was not in their hearts, and they tried to make up for what they lacked inwardly, by putting on outward forms.

They could be haughty and cruel; they could be selfish and proud; they could be unkind to the poor, and unjust to the widow and the fatherless; they could cherish hatred, and sometimes even murder. And as an offset they did a thousand useless things that the Lord never asked them to do.

They hated Jesus because he was pure in heart, and his goodness made them seem wicked — just as they were. They tried to show that Jesus was a sinful man because he healed the sick on the Sabbath day.

At one time, Jesus healed a man at the pool of Bethesda, and told him to take up his bed, and walk. When the Pharisees saw what he was doing, they claimed that he was breaking the Sabbath. Now this poor man had been a cripple for almost forty years.

On another Sabbath, while passing through a field of grain, the disciples shelled out some of the grain in their hands, and ate it. The proud Pharisees,

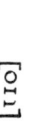

The Disciples Plucking Corn.

[110]

who were always on the watch, said to Jesus, "Why do they on the Sabbath day that which is not lawful?"

Now the disciples had been a long time without food, and it was cruel to keep them from eating a little of the grain. Jesus told the fault-finding Jews that the Sabbath was made for man. It was intended for a blessing, not for a burden.

Christ was one with the Father in creating the world and in setting apart the seventh day as the Sabbath. Should he not know how it ought to be kept? God is merciful and kind, and he wants all his children to be so too. This is the lesson Jesus taught.

One Sabbath, as Jesus was passing along, he saw a man who was born blind. He spat on the ground, made clay of the spittle, rubbed the clay on the man's eyes, and told him to go and wash in the pool of Siloam. When the man had washed, he could see as well as any one.

Now instead of being glad that this poor man could see, the Pharisees were angry when they found that Jesus had healed him. They told him that Jesus could not be a man of God, because he did not keep the Sabbath. But some said, "How can a man that is a sinner do such miracles?"

Jesus taught that it is right to do good and to heal the sick on the Sabbath. Their great need makes it right to help them. It is an act of mercy to do for them. The need of the lame man and the blind man was great, and so was that of the hungry disciples.

[112] JESUS AND THE WOMAN OF SAMARIA.

Jesus at Jacob's Well.

TEXT.— "There cometh a woman of Samaria to draw water: Jesus saith unto her, Give me to drink." John 4 : 7.

JESUS was on his way to Galilee, and his path led through the country of Samaria. It was about noon when he and his disciples reached the lovely valley of Shechem.

In this valley was the city of Sychar, and outside the gates of the city was a well, called the well of Jacob. Jesus being weary and footsore, sat down by the well to rest.

Now the Jews and the Samaritans were not friendly to each other. They would not even eat together, or take a cup of water from each other.

As Jesus sat there by the well, a woman of Samaria came to draw water. All the time she was filling her jar she did not seem to notice Jesus. This was because she could see that he was a Jew.

But as she turned to go, Jesus asked her to give him a drink. But she asked him why he spoke to her, since the Jews would have no dealings with the Samaritans.

Jesus said, "If thou knewest the gift of God, and who it is that saith to thee, Give me to drink, thou wouldest have asked of him, and he would have given thee living water."

The woman thought he claimed a good deal for himself, and so she said, "Art thou greater than our father Jacob?" Jesus said, "Whosoever drinketh of this water shall thirst again: but whosoever drinketh of the water that I shall give him shall never thirst."

The woman could see that it was not the water of the well, that Jesus had offered to give her, and she began to wonder at him. But she did not wish him to know her thoughts, and so she said, "Sir, give me this water, that I thirst not, neither come hither to draw."

Jesus then told her to go and call her husband; but she said, "I have no husband." Jesus wanted to show her that he could read her thoughts, and that he knew all about her; so he told her many things about her past life. Then she said, "Sir, I perceive that thou art a prophet."

Now she had done some very wrong things in her life, and did not want to talk about them; so she asked Jesus if all people ought to go to Jerusalem to worship.

Jesus told her that the time had come when men could worship God anywhere, if they worshiped in spirit and in truth. They must have their hearts in their worship. It is the spirit in which we come to God, and not the place, that makes our worship pleasing to him.

The woman then said, "I know that the Messiah cometh, which is called Christ; when he is come, he will tell us all things." The proper time had now come, and Jesus told her that he was the Christ.

The woman knew that her only hope of being forgiven, and of being saved at last, was in Christ, the coming Saviour; and she did really hope that this might be he. In her joy she left her water-pot, and ran into the town, saying, "Come, see a man, which told me all things which ever I did: is not this the Christ?"

In the meantime, the disciples, who had gone into the town to buy food, returned. And when they saw Jesus talking so freely with a Samaritan, they could not think what it meant. They urged him to take something to eat; but he said, "I have meat to eat that ye know not of."

His joy at giving the true gospel to those Samaritans was so great that he forgot his hunger. It was more than food or drink to him to be doing the works of love and mercy that he had come to the earth to do.

When the people of the city heard the woman's story, many of them believed on Jesus as the Christ. They were anxious to talk with him, and wanted him to stay with them. So he stayed two days; and many more believed on him after hearing his wise and comforting words.

And they said to the woman, "Now we believe, not because of thy saying: for we have heard him ourselves, and know that this is indeed the Christ, **the Saviour of the world.**"

The Need of Prayer.

TEXT.— "In everything by prayer and supplication with thanksgiving let your requests be made known unto God. Philippians 4:6.

THE Lord asks us to come to him in prayer. We may tell him all our trials, all our sorrows. It will bring us near to him, where he can help us.

We must feel our need of him. We must tell him that our troubles are too hard for us; that our only hope is in him. Then he will give us comfort and peace, the sweetest we can ever know.

God knows all about us before we tell him. He is always ready to give us help. But he must help us in his own way; for that is the only right way. This he cannot do till we cast all our care upon him.

We must trust to God to care for us. He wants to fill our hearts with love; but so long as selfishness rules in us, there is no room for him. Selfishness and the Spirit of God cannot dwell together.

How much better to turn out self, and let in the love of God. Jesus says, "If a man love me, he will keep my words; and my father will love him, and we will come unto him, and make our abode with him."

We must ask for God's blessing; ask for his strength; ask for his wisdom. Above all, we must ask for his Holy Spirit to guide us; for it brings all other blessings with it. We may have it by asking for it. Jesus has said:—

"Ask, and it shall be given you; seek, and ye shall find; knock, and it shall be opened unto you."

Men seek after the riches of this world, which soon pass away. Let us seek after heavenly treasures that never fade. Men who seek after worldly riches do not always find them; but we have God's word that if we seek after his riches, we shall find.

But there is one thing we must not forget. We must believe that God will do just what he says he will. "What things soever ye desire, when ye pray, believe that ye receive them, and ye shall have them."

God will surely answer our prayers. If he does not give us just what we think we need,—if we do not get exactly what we ask for,—it is because he has something better for us. He knows what we need better than we do, and will do for us the best that can be done.

None of us know how to pray just as we ought to; but Jesus has promised to teach us, and to plead for us. He who has given his life for us will not neglect us at the throne of grace. The prayer of the humblest man will come before God in just as good form as that of the greatest scholar.

The Bible says we must "watch unto prayer," be "instant in prayer," and "continue in prayer." God's true children pray much. They ask his help and his care in everything. They carry the spirit of prayer with them all the time.

We can lift up our hearts to God in prayer at any time and in every place. The Lord looks upon the heart, and not upon our words only. He reads our thoughts, and hears the silent prayer just as surely as though we spoke aloud.

But it is better to pray in words when we can. God gave us the power of speech, and likes to hear us use it in talking to him.

When Jesus was upon the earth, he felt the need of prayer. He was truly the Son of God; but he had taken upon himself our human nature, and had human wants. He could suffer pain and hunger, as we do. It is said of him that he was a "man of sorrows, and acquainted with grief."

This does not mean that our Lord was not cheerful, but that he could be touched with sorrow and grief, and knows how to pity us when we suffer in the same way. Yes, Jesus, our Master, prayed. He sometimes stayed away alone all night, thinking and praying,— talking to his Father in heaven.

And if he needed to pray, how much more do we. We, who are so poor and needy,— who cannot put away our own sins, or make ourselves any better, without help from above. Jesus is waiting to hear us, and to present our prayers at the great white throne in heaven. He says:—

"Behold, I stand at the door, and knock; if any man hear my voice, and open the door, I will come in to him, and will sup with him, and he with me."

Jesus Riding into Jerusalem.

TEXT.— "Hosanna to the Son of David : Blessed is he that cometh in the name of the Lord." Matthew 21 : 9.

OVER the Mount of Olives, and about three miles from Jerusalem, was the little town of Bethany. Here was the home of Lazarus and his two sisters, Martha and Mary. It was a quiet place, and Jesus liked to stop there sometimes for a little rest.

Jesus loved this family, and they all loved him. He had done much for them, and they felt that they could not do enough in return. At one time Lazarus had been very sick. The sisters sent for Jesus to come and heal him; but when Jesus reached the place, Lazarus had been dead four days.

Mary and Martha mourned much, that he had not come sooner. But Jesus asked them to take him to the tomb where Lazarus was buried. When they came to the place, Jesus cried, "Lazarus, come forth," and he came out, bound in his grave-clothes.

Not long after this, Jesus came to Bethany again, and stayed there over the Sabbath. Now while Jesus was eating in the house of Simon, Mary came and anointed his feet with some very costly ointment. When some found fault with her for wasting anything so precious, Jesus told them to let her alone; she was anointing him for his burial.

This was only six days before the passover; and

JESUS RIDING INTO JERUSALEM.

at that passover Jesus was to be put to death. Now when the people who had come up to Jerusalem to the passover heard that Jesus was at Bethany, many came out to see him, and to see Lazarus also, because Jesus had raised him from the dead.

The next day, Sunday, when Jesus went to Jerusalem, a great company of people went with him. Many people from Jerusalem also came out to meet him, when they saw the procession moving along the side of the Mount of Olives, over against the city.

The procession attracted much attention; for Jesus was riding on a colt, and the people were throwing palm branches, and even their garments, in the road before him, and crying, "Blessed is the king of Israel that cometh in the name of the Lord."

Jesus had never before allowed the people to treat him as a king. He had always said, "My kingdom is not of this world." He had come to the earth to save sinners; and not be a king in Jerusalem.

Before he came to the earth, he was a king in heaven; that was so much better than being king on the earth. He would never have left his glorious kingdom above to come here and reign as earthly kings reign. His kingdom is in the hearts of men, and for them he was willing to give his life.

But Jesus did not intend to exalt himself. After looking at the beautiful buildings of the temple, and talking about them to his disciples, he went quietly back to Bethany to spend the night.

THE CRUCIFIXION.

"And I, if I be lifted up from the earth, will draw all men unto me." John 12 : 32.

The Ascension.

TEXT.—"And when he had spoken these things, while they beheld, he was taken up; and a cloud received him out of their sight." Acts 1:9.

JESUS had now finished his work as a man here on this earth. The devil had tempted him in every way in which he can tempt us; but Jesus did not commit even one little sin. He was as poor as the poorest man that ever lived on the earth. And he finally suffered and died on the cross.

This was to teach the poorest, that God will save the poor man as well as the rich man, for Christ was poor. And when we are tempted in any way, we must remember that Christ was tempted in just that way, for the Bible says he was tempted in all points, just as we are. And if we suffer for doing as God has told us to do, we know that Jesus has suffered more than we can. We must also remember that Jesus has said, "Lo, I am with you always." And if we are poor, or are tempted, or suffer for Jesus, we can be glad to know that Jesus is with us all through our trouble, and is bearing it with us.

Well, Jesus was having a last talk with his disciples. He told them that when he went away, he would send his Holy Spirit to lead and guide them. When he had told them this he was taken up from them into heaven. And while they were looking up toward

THE ASCENSION.

heaven, where Jesus had gone, two angels came and stood beside them, to comfort them for the loss of the dear Jesus who had been with them for so long. And the angels said to the disciples, "Ye men of Galilee, why stand ye gazing up into heaven? This same Jesus, which is taken up from you into heaven, shall so come in like manner as ye have seen him go into heaven."

This was a blessed promise, and it is as good to us now as it was to them then. The promise was that "this same Jesus" whom they had known and loved so long, is to come to this earth again. And those who love him when he comes, will see him come just as the disciples saw him when he went away, for the Bible says so.

And when he comes the next time he will gather together all who have been good on the earth, and then he will go back to heaven again and take them with him. Jesus is now in heaven preparing a place for us, so that when it is time for him to come to this earth again, to get all who love him, he will have a place ready for them. He says, "I go to prepare a place for you. And if I go and prepare a place for you, I will come again, and receive you unto myself; that where I am, there ye may be also."

We all want a place in that beautiful city that Jesus went to prepare, but if we have it, we must love and serve him here. If we do, he will say, "Well done, good and faithful servant."

A LITTLE CHILD SHALL LEAD THEM.

A Little Child Shall Lead Them.

Text.—"The wolf also shall dwell with the lamb, and the leopard shall lie down with the kid; and the calf and the young lion and the fatling together; and a little child shall lead them." Isaiah 11:6.

WHEN God made this world, it was very beautiful. It did not have the rough mountains, and barren deserts, and swamps full of disease. No, it was all perfect, for God said it was "very good." Everything that grew out of the ground was good, and there were no thistles, nor briars, nor weeds. The beasts and birds were not as they are now. The great lions and tigers were gentle and kind, like the kittens and dogs you love to play with.

But when man sinned and became wicked, God could not bless the earth any more, but made the thistles grow where the roses had grown before, and briars came up in the place of the beautiful vines. And then the flood came, and great earthquakes, which tore up the beautiful earth, and made the rough mountains. All these things were to show to men how bad sin is, and that it made them worse, and the earth which was made for them.

The animals, too, were changed. Before sin came they loved man, and were glad to obey him. But when Adam sinned and did not obey God, then the animals ceased to love and obey him. They were changed, and have become fierce and wild, and the strong animals will kill the weak ones, and even man is not safe where they are. So this earth is not good and beautiful as it was when God made it, and man is not good and happy and well, but is wicked and sad.

But this will not be so always. God has promised that he will make this earth all over new, and it will be good and beautiful again, as it was before Adam sinned. The wicked people will be burned up, and then those who have loved the dear Saviour, and whose sins have all been forgiven, will come back to the earth to live. And then everything will be good and happy again, as it was when the earth was first made.

And Jesus is making a wonderful city in heaven, and in it he is making beautiful homes for us. Jesus has told us about these homes in John 14 : 2, 3. This beautiful city is called the New Jerusalem, and Jesus will bring it down from heaven to the new earth, and it will be our home forever. How large do you think this city will be? If you will read the twenty-first chapter of Revelation, you will learn all about it, and how it will come down from heaven to the earth. And you will find that the city is one thousand, five hundred miles around it. There is no city in the world so large as this one.

And then all will be peace and happiness everywhere; and the animals will love and obey man, and the little child will play with the lions and savage tigers, and all will be joyful together, as you see in the picture.